175 BEST DATE IDEAS

175 Best Date Ideas | the ultimate bucket list of dates for couples

Copyright © 2016 Alida Quittschreiber | TheRealisticMama.com

Stock Photography DollarPhotoClub.com | DimaGroshev

Cover Design and Illustrations by Inspired-Help.com

Publishing Services by MelindaMartin.me

175 BEST DATE IDEAS

the ultimate bucket list of dates for couples

Alida Quittschreiber

INTRODUCTION

Don't go on another boring date! With these 175 dates you're sure to find plenty you love. Whether you've been together for just a week or for 25 years, these dates will make unforgettable memories, spark that extra love and help you fall in love all over again.

Challenge yourself to choose the dates that push you outside your comfort zone or are something you wouldn't have thought to do yourself. And if you're really brave, add all 175 dates to your bucket list and work your way through every one, checking them off as you go!

You will find all kinds of ideas and suggestions here! Some will inspire you to be goofy together and some will create more serious, heart-to-heart moments for you to enjoy.

Next to each date you'll find either a "Go Out" doodle or a "Stay In" doodle. These help make it even easier to plan ahead.

Are you ready to make some unforgettable memories? See if you can accomplish all 175 dates!

What are you waiting for?

SHARE PICTURES AS YOU GO!

Show us your selfies and photos from your dates.

Use the hashtag

#175DATEIDEAS

on Instagram, Facebook, or Twitter.

SMASH BOOK INTRO

This idea is optional, but highly recommended!

HERE'S HOW IT WORKS:

- We've provided some extra pages, in the back of the book, where you can smash, glue, tape or paper clip any flat memories you collect during your dates (movie stubs, tickets, scorecards, printed selfies, and photos from your dates).

- Date #5 will explain more about what a Smash Book is and then throughout the book we will remind you to save small keepsakes from the dates to "smash" in your pages.

- There are also some "specialty pages" in the Smash Book portion, like creating a bucket list, which corresponds to a specific date in the book.

- And finally, don't forget to leave any fun notes you want to be sure not to forget, like, "We weren't sure about the selfie date but for whatever reason decided to give it a whirl and, goodness, it is now one of our favorite all time memories with each other. There was so much laughter and giggling; I thought I was going to explode!" Or maybe you learned something new about your hubby. Make a note, "I can't believe I've been with this guy for 10 years and didn't know he was deathly afraid of snakes."

Note: If you have the ebook version of this book you can either download and print the Smash Book pages at

http://therealisticmama.com/smash-pages

or find an empty notebook to start your Smash Book. An empty notebook is also a great option for those that are extra crafty and see themselves needing more room!

MONEY SAVING TIPS

Most of the dates in this book are inexpensive, some even free, but there are a few that cost a little extra. Here are some easy ways you can save up for those dates:

- Create a jar (or envelope) that is specifically for your Date Night Fund!

- Save every $5 bill. You'll be surprised at how quickly it will add into a nice sum!

- Ask for $10-$20 cash back each trip to the grocery store. Chances are you won't even notice this in your monthly budget and your date fund will quickly grow!

- Lastly, as silly as it sounds, save up every single coin you can. Once you have a nice little stack of coins, you can take them to a bank or make a date of counting and rolling the coins.

TIPS FOR COUPLES WITH KIDS

Have kids? No problem! We've got you covered, too.

The "Stay In" section of this book will be your go-to for nights when you can't find a sitter. Just because you can't leave the house doesn't mean you can't have a date night! Some weeks, just finding an hour to reconnect can make all the difference in a relationship. In some way or another, try to find at least an hour each week for just the two of you.

For "Go Out" dates, you will need someone to take care of the kids. Hiring a babysitter is always a good option, but if you're on a tight budget, finding another mom friend who can exchange nights of watching kids works wonderfully. It is a play date for the kids and a date night all rolled into one!

Many of these date ideas would also work well as a daddy-daughter or mom-son date, too. While that isn't the focus of this book, feel free to use it as inspiration.

We've also made plenty of other suggestions for you throughout the book.

175 BEST DATE IDEAS

1

FOOD CRAWL

This date will be a full night, and so much fun! It's simple - just get appetizers, dinner, drinks and dessert at four different places.

2

DISPOSABLE CAMERA DATE

Buy a disposable camera and take 8 goofy pictures together. Develop them that same day and buy an 8 frame collage so you can frame the pictures that night! For extra fun, change outfits a couple of times on the go. Be creative and have fun!

PLAY INDOOR GOLF

 STAY IN

Set up a mini course in your living room, down the hall and to the kitchen. Use a plastic cup or a small cardboard box on its side as the 'hole'. If the ball touches the wall, it counts as an extra stroke. Take turns setting up new routes and placing obstacles in the way!

Note: If you don't have clubs, search for a used set at yard sales or a thrift store.

4

GO COUCH BROWSING

 GO OUT

Visit furniture stores to test out couches and recliners. Sit on a comfy couch and chat for a while, then go to the next couch. Don't miss the fancy recliners with all the special features!

5

MAKE A SMASH BOOK

STAY IN

Make your very first Date Night Smash Book! You basically just smash/glue/tape random memories from your dates into the "Smash Book" section at the back of this book.

There are no rules, just a collection of memories all gathered together in one place. Start the book off with a love letter to each other (write them directly on pages #106 and 107 or paper clip them in). Then, throughout this book we'll remind you to save fun memories (like movie stubs, tickets, and scorecards) to smash onto the pages. Develop a few pictures from the photo shoot date (#10) and selfie date (#174) and include those in the back, too!

Use the Smash Book to record memories from your dates all year long, and enjoy it together at the end of the year. See Smash Book Intro (at the front of this book) for more information.

SMASH BOOK !

#175DATEIDEAS

11

6

RESTAURANT ROULETTE

Go out to eat somewhere you've never been. Do a quick internet search for restaurants in your area, then write down 3-5 you've never tried. Put them in bowl and draw a restaurant at random and that's where you'll go.
Dress up and enjoy the night!

7

PLAY DING DONG DITCH

Can you remember doing this as a kid? For a fun and more responsible twist, leave gifts on your friends' porches - ring the doorbell then run and hide while they discover the surprises!

8

$10 "CHOOSE ANYTHING" SHOPPING DATE

This one's so flexible it can be turned into several different date nights. The rules are simple: starting with $10 you'll pick a store and each of you gets $5 to spend on something to enjoy together that night! Any store choice will work. Some of our favorite suggestions are:

• Movie Rental Store — one person picks the movie; the other chooses snacks!

• Craft Store — endless possibilities, from model airplanes to canvases and paint. Remember, you each get to use your $5 however you want!

• Grocery Store — choose ingredients for a meal (or pick your favorite ready-made desserts).

• Dollar Store — $10 goes pretty far here!

9

GAME NIGHT WITH A TWIST

 STAY IN

Start with a favorite board game you already own and create a brand new game with your own rules. You have to use the same board and all the pieces, but the rules of the game are entirely up to you. Get creative!

10

PHOTO SHOOT

 GO OUT

Do you remember getting your engagement & wedding pictures taken? So much love, laughter, and fun . . . why not recreate these moments for an anniversary memory? If you have the means to hire a professional photographer, go for it! Otherwise, you probably have a friend or two who would be willing to take them for you. (If you rely on a friend's services, try offering to take photos of them in return; or bring them home-baked goodies as payment!)

11

COOK A MEAL TOGETHER

This is one you can repeat many times. If you're on a tight budget, consider a meal that will provide lunch leftovers later in the week. Or, if you can afford it, try something fancy and new! Either way, don't forget the tablecloth, candles, and favorite date music.

12

BOWLING

Many bowling alleys have themed nights. Research ahead of time to find a place that's extra fun!

PICNIC DATE

The good, old-fashioned picnic is always a winner. Plan plenty of time so you can really enjoy catching up and chatting. Pick a park you haven't visited before or drive until you find a picnic table in a more obscure, but totally cool place. Don't worry about making a coordinated meal — each of you pack 3 favorite food items (surprise each other)!

14

FOAM DART GUN WAR

You can often find foam dart guns inexpensively at thrift stores or even toy stores. Dress in all black, sneak around the house, and see who is a better shot! Budget version: take two socks and make them into a ball. Use them as "grenades" to launch at each other! If you're bold, head out to a local park for this epic battle so you can really embrace your inner ninja.

CHEESY PHOTO BOOTH

Try a mall or local arcade to find an old school photo booth. If you have multiple kiosks in your town, make it a progressive date and stop at a few! Bonus: these will also make a great addition to your date night Smash Book.

MOVIES & POPCORN ON THE SOFA

Turn on a favorite movie, pop some popcorn, and snuggle up! Sometimes the simplest dates can be the most fun. If you want to add something new, try different recipes for homemade popcorn and pair with a variety of wines.

17

CARDS AT THE COFFEE SHOP

Go to a coffee shop with a deck of cards. Play simple games and chat, or learn the rules to a new game together.

18

TAKE FREE ONLINE PERSONALITY TESTS

There are so many great options out there; so explore and find one that appeals to both of you. A good starting point is a Myers-Briggs Type Indicator. Once you find your type, research information about your personality -- what jobs fit this personality, what the parenting style tends to be, strengths and weaknesses as a spouse, etc. This can help provide a good place to start talking about communication in your relationship and conflicts you've faced in the past. Print the results or jot down a note and add it to your Smash Book!

INDOOR CAMPOUT

Make a bed of blankets or sleeping bags in your living room or even set up a small tent for the authentic experience. Make indoor s'mores or other favorite camp foods and start a fire, if you are lucky enough to have a fireplace. Don't forget to turn off the lights and just use candles or flashlights!

BINGO

Many towns have community centers with Bingo night.

Tip: Wanna volunteer together? Playing Bingo at a retirement home with elderly residents is a great way to socialize and bring joy to others.

21

WATER FIGHT

Grab some squirt guns and water balloons at the dollar store and head to a local park, or your own backyard! For some extra fun put food coloring or tie-dye in the water.

22

TAKE A DRIVE TOGETHER

Listen to your favorite radio station and enjoy some quality conversation!

Tip: Find some back roads to travel so the driver isn't too distracted by traffic and stoplights.

23

DIY NIGHT

Check Pinterest and select a DIY craft that you both would enjoy. Then, head to the craft or hardware store together and buy all the supplies for your project. Don't forget to snap a photo of the finished project for your Smash Book!

24

EXERCISE TOGETHER

Do something you both love, or take turns choosing what to do. You could head to the gym and hit the treadmills, go for a swim, sign up for a workout class, or find a free online video and workout in the living room together.

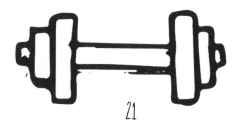

25

BACKYARD MOVIE

STAY IN

On a warm night, throw a blanket on the grass and bring your laptop outside. Watch a movie under the stars. It's like your very own drive-in!

26

WINE TASTING

GO OUT

If you have an entire day or weekend, try to visit several wineries. Otherwise, choose a winery you've never been and buy a special bottle after your tasting to enjoy at a future date. Save your tasting menu to put in your Smash Book.

27

MAKE A VISION BOARD TOGETHER

Buy a large poster board and use it to create a collage of all your biggest dreams. Dream together and remember, money is no object. Dare each other to dream as big as you can - you may learn new things about what excites and inspires your spouse.

28

HIKING AT A NATIONAL OR STATE PARK

Do your research ahead of time, and find a hike that is the perfect distance. Many National and State Parks have great picnic spots or historic sites to enjoy as well.

29

PIZZA NIGHT

STAY IN

If you're on a budget, keep it simple: no soda, no breadsticks, just a good ole' pizza! Or, if you're feeling up to cooking, make your own pizza at home together and load on all your favorite toppings. Does your husband (or you!) have a sweet tooth? Homemade dessert pizza is always a great option -- a sugar cookie crust with fruit toppings is so yummy!

30

WATCH A LIVE SPORTING EVENT

GO OUT

Can't afford a pro game? Check out a local college (or even high school) for cheaper tickets! And don't forget to branch out - try wrestling, roller derby, or hockey to change things up.

31

BOARD GAME NIGHT

Play an old favorite or pick out a new one together. If you get stumped on what to play, ask family or friends for suggestions and borrow their favorite.

32

BAKING DAY

Bake up as many recipes as you can, and make the house smell amazing! Make enough to enjoy together, some to freeze for future dates, and a few extras to give to friends or neighbors.

33

FRISBEE GOLF

Even in small towns, many parks or universities will have a frisbee golf course available. If not, just choose your own "holes" each time - a tree, bush, lamppost, etc. You can compete against each other or play as a team, rotating every other throw. Then try to beat your own score.

34

ICE CREAM OR FROYO

Head out late, and enjoy your treat in the car together or at the park.

35

DANCE LESSONS

A spouse is a built-in dancing partner! There are so many different styles of dance from which to choose. Often local universities have a dance club that offers lessons. After a few lessons, flaunt your skills by dressing up and going out for a dancing date!

36

CHILDHOOD MEMORIES

Sit together and go through old boxes of keepsakes from your childhood. Share your funniest stories and favorite memories.

NATURE WALK

Check out your closest botanical garden or other special feature, like a waterfall or riverside. See who can identify flowers, wildlife, and trees; or pack a sketch pad to sit together and draw the prettiest thing you see. When you get home, add your sketches to your Smash Book.

PLAY VIDEO GAMES

The best games to play together are ones that get you dancing or active. Or try your hand at your husband's favorite game . . . you may not be as bad as you think and you might figure out what he loves so much about it!

39

PARK HOPPING

GO OUT

Enjoy swings at the first park, slides at the next, and finish with a seesaw at the last one. Chat in the car while you drive between parks and take photos of each other as you go!

40

LIVING ROOM PICNIC

STAY IN

Pack a picnic and spread a blanket on the living room floor. Enjoy picnic foods and reclining while you eat.

BANANA SPLIT SELF-SERVE BAR

This is an easy dessert to make together! Personalize it for a date night by choosing your own toppings. Layer together: ice cream, bananas, chocolate chips, and whipped cream. Top with your favorite sweets . . . sprinkles, a cherry, mini marshmallows, chocolate syrup, caramel syrup, etc. Enjoy with a cup of coffee and chat about your favorite desserts as a child and the special memories they evoke.

WINE UNDER THE STARS

Sit outside with a glass of wine and watch the stars together — the peace and beauty of being outside is a perfect setting for intimate conversations.

43

ATTEND A CONCERT

GO OUT

Buy tickets to a concert featuring a band you both enjoy.
Or if you don't want to spend money on tickets, find a local
band who has a free cover.

44

BREAKFAST IN BED

STAY IN

**Bring the laptop and watch a morning movie, or just sit
and chat while you eat breakfast in bed.** Make some fun
heart-shaped food to add a little romantic touch! Cookie
cutters can make heart-shaped toast and fried eggs in a cinch.
Or, if you're not a morning person, making baked oatmeal the
night before (unbaked but ready to go in a 9x13 pan) is a great
option. That way you can get up, quickly throw it in the oven,
and slip back into bed while it bakes. Don't forget the coffee,
too. Most coffee pots have presets, so it's already brewing
when you wake up!

MINI GOLF

Don't forget to keep score! You might be surprised how competitive your partner gets. Hang on to the scorecards and tuck it in to your Smash Book after the date!

46

MESSY TWISTER©

Put on white shirts & get ready for some messy fun. All you need for this is a Twister© game and paint that corresponds with each color. Drip corresponding paint into each Twister© circle and start the game! Enjoy getting messy together, and save the shirts to remind you of how much fun you had.

SPONTANEOUS ROAD TRIP

Figure out how much time you have available for your date, and start driving until you've reached 1/3 of that time. (For a 3-hour date, drive for 1 hour!) Then spend 1/3 of your date at that location, and 1/3 driving home. No fair planning ahead - you just have to figure out what to do when you get there. You may have to get creative if your time runs out while you are in the middle of nowhere!

HOMEMADE HOT CHOCOLATE

This is perfect for winter or really any time of year! Make this delicious recipe together. (No cheating and buying the store-bought stuff. Making it together is half the fun!) Then bundle up and go sit outside while you sip. If it's too chilly even with bundling up, stay inside and tuck a blanket around yourselves instead.

BEST EVER HOT CHOCOLATE RECIPE

This recipe is seriously the best. It's not gritty. It's not watery. Instead, think smooth, creamy and absolutely perfect for a date night!

INGREDIENTS

- 1/4 cup maple syrup
- 1/4 cup water
- 3 cups whole milk
- 1/4 cup cocoa powder
- 1 Tbsp. vanilla extract

DIRECTIONS

1. Combine maple syrup and water in a medium sized saucepan over medium-low heat — whisk till combined.
2. Add milk and cocoa powder and whisk until hot.
3. Remove from heat and add vanilla extract.
4. Now quickly whip up some whipped cream (see recipe below!).
5. Pour hot chocolate into mugs and top with whipped cream and marshmallows!

Makes 3-4 cups, which is perfect because, chances are, you'll want a refill!

HOMEMADE WHIPPED CREAM

INGREDIENTS

- 1/4 cup heavy whipping cream
- 1 tsp. maple syrup

Double the recipe if you like a lot of whipped cream!

DIRECTIONS

1. Use a hand mixer and whisk the 2 ingredients until they turn into whipped cream. We turned our hand mixer up to power 3 and it took about 3-5 minutes.
2. That's it! ENJOY!

49

THRIFT STORE OUTFIT DINNER

There are so many things you can find here! Before your next date, visit a local thrift store together and choose an outfit for the other person. Your spouse can try it on, but you get the final say.

50

RE-DECORATE A ROOM IN YOUR HOUSE

 STAY IN

This could be a date that extends over several evenings. Start by getting inspired - watch your favorite home improvement show together, or search through Pinterest for styles and ideas you like. Then start planning - choose paint colors, research any new furniture you might want to purchase, and take some shopping trips for new bedding, frames, vases, etc. Finally, block off a weekend day or evening to tackle the project! Paint together; then decorate with the items you've chosen. If re-decorating isn't in the budget right now, choose a room and rearrange the furniture together. You can also switch out seasonal decor or update family photos in frames!

51

DART PAINTING

 STAY IN

Fill water balloons with paint. Pin them to a canvas and head outside to shoot some darts at those balloons!

VOLUNTEER TOGETHER

Serve a meal at a local homeless shelter and bring some warm blankets or clothing to donate. Or find other opportunities to serve others in your community, and do it alongside each other.

MAKE COSTUMES

Choose a couples' Halloween costume idea, and help each other design and make them. A trip to the thrift store will likely be involved, and remember that safety pins are a perfectly acceptable alternative to sewing! You might be surprised at your spouse's creativity. Making the costumes together beforehand will make the night even more memorable!

54

FLY KITES

The windy season of fall is perfect for this. You can easily find a kite online or at a local store; but for extra fun, try to make your own! A simple internet search will provide instructions.

55

FLEA MARKET UPCYCLE

Go to the flea market and find an old item that you can fix up today! Either work on a project together, or compete on separate projects. Don't forget to take before and after shots to see the improvement.

GOURMET CHEF SHOW

Cook a fancy, gourmet meal together. Pull out your camera to document the process, just like your favorite cooking show. Don't forget to decorate the plates with the food; a sprig of mint, a twisted orange slice, drizzles of chocolate and more. If you are needing inspiration, just check out Pinterest - not only will you find recipes, but also ideas on how to design each plate into a work of art!

TRAMPOLINE PARK

This fun, trendy activity isn't just for kids! Get ready for lots of laughter, falling down, and maybe sore muscles in the morning.

58

CHORE SWITCH-EROO

STAY IN

Trade off the tasks that you normally do. For example, take an afternoon to get your house ready for winter together – clean out gutters, rake leaves, prune your bushes and trees. Choose one task you normally do, and show him how to do it, and vice versa. Maybe you can climb the ladder to clean gutters, and he can prune your rose bushes. Do it together and enjoy learning from your spouse! This can be outdoor or indoor chores, house maintenance tasks. You name it – just do it together.

59

FARMER'S MARKET DATE

GO OUT

Shop at a local Farmer's Market in the morning and buy ingredients to make a new recipe for lunch. Bonus points if you make up a brand new recipe together!

60

DIY WREATH

Make a DIY monogram wreath for your front door. Or instead of a wreath, get a blank wooden letter for your last name and decorate it. Choose decor elements that you both love or a favorite flower from your wedding day.

61

BASKETBALL DATE

Get day passes to your local gym and play basketball together. Whether you're an excellent athlete or you have to make granny shots, just have fun with it!

SUNSET WATCHING

Find a scenic overlook nearby or another favorite spot where you can watch the sunset together. Some homes are built such that sitting on the roof on a blanket is the perfect spot (just don't let the kids see you crawl out there!). Early birds? Catch a sunrise together instead! Try to do this once each season of the year - you'll be amazed at how different a sunset can look because of the time of year.

63

SURPRISE DATES

This will actually turn into 2 dates. Each of you pick a night to plan a surprise date. Prepare a date that best fits your sweetheart and his or her favorite things to do. Don't tell the other where you're going . . . just get in the car and drive to the location (or direct him where to drive without giving it away).

GO TO A WATER PARK OR LOCAL POOL

Soak up the sun together on a lounge chair. Swim laps, or go down as many slides as you can.

RECREATE A MEMORY

If you're already married, you can recreate your honeymoon. If you're not yet married, try to recreate your first date. It can be as simple or extravagant as you want. Example: If your honeymoon was in a tropical location, maybe make some homemade margaritas to enjoy together, or head to the closest beach and chat about your favorite memories from your honeymoon (or first date).

66

ADVENTURE DATE

Ziplining, skydiving, whitewater rafting . . . choose
something big and adventurous that you can do together!
Maybe it's one of your big, scary, bucket list items.

67

GET TO KNOW YOU

**Whether you've been together for a day or 25 years,
there's always more you can learn about each other!**
Prepare a bunch of questions ahead of time and slip them
in an envelope. When date time comes, take turns choosing
questions from the envelope. I bet you'll be surprised with
some of the answers you hear and the conversations you have
in between!

HERE ARE SOME QUESTIONS TO START THE CONVERSATION:

- What's your favorite childhood memory?

- What was your favorite childhood home?

- What's your favorite food? Favorite book? Favorite movie? (Ask these simple questions too, because it may have changed since you last talked about it!)

- If you could have any superhero power, what would you choose?

- If you could build anything in our backyard, what would you build?

- What does your dream house look like?

- If you were stranded on a desert island, what 3 things would you take with you?

- If you could only use one word to describe yourself, what would it be?

- If you could be invisible for one day, what would you do?

- What is your favorite all time memory?

- If you had one million dollars, how would you spend it?

Note: This is a great stay-at-home date if you have kids and can't find a babysitter. Get the kids to bed, grab a tub of ice cream, 2 spoons and your envelope of questions.

68

APPLE OR BLUEBERRY PICKING

Go apple picking at a local orchard or blueberry picking at a local blueberry farm! Find some new recipes to try with the fruit you bring home.

69

CAR DATE WITH KIDS IN TOW

Have kids? Here's a way you can sneak in a date and some alone time when you can't find a babysitter. Get the kids in their pj's and ready for bed, then put them in the van to watch a video and drive. If you time it right, they should fall asleep quickly and you can grab a fast food dinner, park and talk and reconnect. You can also bring a laptop or use your phones to watch a movie in the car once you park. Maybe it will be easiest to just park in your own driveway once the kids are asleep! With it so quiet, you'll almost forget that you aren't alone.

Note: If you don't have kids, you can still have a movie date in the car, just grab your laptop or phone, run through a drive through and park anywhere you like!

70

COOKING CLASS

Have a blast taking a cooking class together. They are often offered at the more high-end kitchen stores. You'll make your own meal under the direction of a chef and then go home with the recipes so you can practice again and recreate the meal. The best part is that you pick the class in advance so you know the menu and what to expect. It's fun to learn new things together and be rewarded with an awesome meal!

71

ICE SKATING

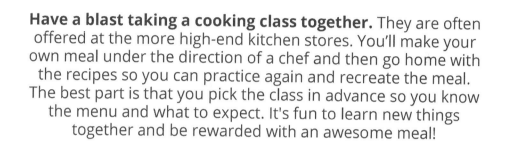

Go ice skating and make sure you bring a thermos of hot chocolate (page 34)! If you're feeling adventurous, try skating backwards or dancing along with the music.

72

POT A PLANT

GO OUT   STAY IN

Choosing plants can be the most fun or most difficult part of this process. Thankfully, most nurseries are pretty good about helping! Have fun choosing plants that both catch your eye and ones you'll be able to keep alive. You can also start a mini herb garden together. There are great options for both indoor and outdoor versions of a mini herb garden. Take turns caring for your new plants and enjoy watching them grow! Some of our favorite low-maintenance indoor plants are aloe, golden pothos, spider plants, geraniums, jade plants, polka-dot plants, and any succulents. Each of these also work well in a shady porch in the summer.

73

WATCH A BROADWAY SHOW

GO OUT

If you are lucky enough to have a large theatre in your city, dress up and splurge on tickets. Otherwise, most towns have a local community theatre group or a high school theatre program that puts on regular shows.

74

RUN (OR WALK) A 5K RACE

You can plan to train a few days each week together, or just show up and do your best the day of the race! Try to find a fun themed race to make it even more memorable.

75

CAMP-OUT IN THE BACKYARD

When the weather is agreeable, pitch a tent in the backyard and have a simple, yet totally fun, camp out together. Turn your phone off or on silent and enjoy some quality time.

76

BE TOURISTS IN YOUR OWN CITY

GO OUT

Head to the visitors center and ask if there are local historic landmarks or must-see museums. Choose one you've never seen and enjoy exploring!

77

LEARN A DANCE ROUTINE AT HOME

STAY IN

Have you ever been at a wedding and wished you could dance along with the crowd? Choose a popular song with a set dance routine and learn it together with a free online video.

78

CREATE A SCAVENGER HUNT

Try searching online to see if there is a ready made map for your town. If not, then find a free photo scavenger hunt online and see how fast you can complete it. Don't forget to add the photos to your Smash Book! If you have more time, you could also put one together with clues based on memories you have or your favorite date locations!

79

80'S THEMED NIGHT

Plan a night themed around the 80's. Choose clothes from that era and head into town and enjoy being goofy together. See if you can find a restaurant or a place to hang out that matches your 80's theme! Another week, go on a 70's themed night!

80

WORK OF ART

Buy two canvases and some paint. Using the same combination of colors, take turns giving each other directions on how to paint his or her piece. To make it extra hard, try to give directions without watching! See if you can accomplish a pair of paintings that look like a set!

81

DOUBLE DATE WITH FRIENDS

To make it even more unique, try to find an older couple, and ask them questions about their relationship and what life was like when they were a young couple (or vice versa if you are an older couple).

82

CHILDHOOD MOVIE NIGHT

Watch one of your favorite videos from childhood and share memories about why you loved it so much.

83

GO TO AN ART MUSEUM

Pick a favorite piece and share why you like it! Many museums have free days, so call ahead. You might also be able to find an art gallery that has special event nights with wine and viewings.

84

DAY ON THE WATER

Find a lake nearby with paddleboats or canoe rentals.
Apply sunscreen and get lost on the water together.

85

MUSIC THROWBACK NIGHT

After the kids are in bed, fix a snack tray and get out your phone or tablet. Look up your favorite music and music videos and enjoy them together. Depending on what era of music you like, you might even pull out some clips of theme songs from old shows or movie soundtracks. Sometimes it becomes a competition on who can find the best/worst for the night! You may even end up dancing around the living room or house.

86

DRIVING RANGE

Head to a driving range and hit a bunch of golf balls together!

87

RELIVE YOUR FAVORITE MOMENTS

Make a list of places you've shared milestones together. Stop by the place he proposed and reminisce about that special day. Swing by the spot of your first kiss and share another kiss, just like you did before. Drive by your first apartment or house together or have dinner at the restaurant of your first date. If your wedding venue hosts public events, plan to attend one and let it rekindle all the memories of your special day.

88

DINNER OF APPETIZERS

Buy wine, cheese, olives, bread, etc. and make some fancy appetizers. Put the kids to bed early, sit down, share the appetizers and have a good talk. Use this time to talk about your feelings, set goals as a couple, or chat about the past and remember back to when you started your relationship.

89

CARD GAME NIGHT

Start by choosing a game at random. Then, whoever wins gets to choose the next game. The winner of that game chooses the next, and so on. Don't choose the same game twice in a row; keep switching it up!

90

BOOKSTORE DATE

Head to your favorite bookstore, choose an old favorite and enjoy some coffee while you read together.

Hint: Most bookstores have comic books or magazines too!

91

MAKE BUCKET LISTS

Make three lists: one for you, one for him, and one list of things you want to both accomplish together. Tape the lists in your Smash Book (page #108) so you can be reminded of them every time you use it. Cross things off as you accomplish them!

92

PLAY LASER TAG

Go with another couple and team up against each other, or play girls vs. guys. You might be surprised with who comes out on top!

93

EXPLORE THE SCIENCE MUSEUM

Many think science centers are geared only towards kids, but they have exhibits that will stretch your mind too! And keep your eyes open for special exhibits or themes that interest you.

94

TEST DRIVE A NEW CAR

Don't go safe and pick a minivan! Choose a car you've always dreamed of owning, or pick one the next level up from what you can afford.

95

GIVE A CARD

Go to a local greeting card store, or a grocery story that has a greeting card aisle. Take some time and each pick the goofiest, funniest card for each other. Exchange the cards, snap a picture with your phone, and return them to the shelf. Use the money you would have spent on the card to buy a candy bar (or two) to enjoy together on the ride home.

96

SWITCH HOUSES WITH ANOTHER COUPLE FOR A NIGHT

Get away from the distractions of your own house so you can focus on each other. Before the other couple arrives, set up your guest room like a bed & breakfast! Then simply trade keys and enjoy your night "away." Who knows - when you arrive you might find chocolates on the bed, or maybe a bottle of champagne!

97

PAINT YOUR OWN

Head to a paint your own pottery shop. Each choose a mug or other item and make it for the other. Take photos while you're there for your Smash Book.

98

BUY SOMETHING FUN TOGETHER

Walk through your favorite stores and browse for items you both would love! Beforehand, decide on a price range, something a little more than you normally spend. If you're on a really tight budget that might be $20; for others it will be $100; for some even more. Decide on one item that you both love that's within that price range but don't buy the item just yet. Snap a picture of the item and head home. Over the next few weeks save a little "here and there" specifically for your item. Decide if you'll save just coins, or maybe $5 a week. Decorate a jar or envelope for the item and keep track of how close you're getting! It's super fun to be able to buy the item after intentionally saving for it. Even if you had the extra cash at the time you browsed, there's something about saving up that adds to the fun.

99

CORN MAZE

Get lost in a corn maze, and put your heads together to find the exit!

100

GO TO THE MOVIES

Find a dollar theater with older movies, or a new theater with recliners. Don't forget the popcorn, and save your ticket stubs for your Smash Book.

101

DEPARTMENT STORE OUTFITS

Go to a department store and choose outfits for each other! If your man doesn't normally wear a suit, it might be fun to have him try one. Guys, be brave - find something daring that you think would make your wife look beautiful.

Tip: Dresses are an easy option, because you don't have to worry about matching pieces. Snap a photo together in your outfits so you have the memory, even if you decide not to buy the outfits.

102

LEARN A NEW INSTRUMENT

If one of you plays an instrument, spend a night teaching the other one a song; or sign up to learn a new instrument together! If you want to stay at home while you learn (which would make it easier if you have kids), consider buying an online course. This could easily turn into multiple dates of choosing new songs and learning together!

Bonus: if you have kids, they can learn using the course too (just not during date night!).

103

GO TO A FESTIVAL

Check your local community calendar for free or inexpensive events. Some examples include: cider pressing, heritage days, vintage markets, music festivals, etc.

104

GET A HOTEL FOR A NIGHT

If it doesn't fit your budget, then save up over several months. If you're flexible on dates, chances are you can get a 3-4 star hotel for a great deal! Consider booking it for a date that's a month or two in advance for even better prices. If you have kids, see if grandma and grandpa, or a trusty friend, can watch the kids for a night.

105

ARCADE GAME NIGHT

For a fun throwback to junior high, head to a local arcade with a jar full of quarters! Play games that are old favorites or learn something new. Don't worry if you are the oldest ones there - focus on each other and it won't matter at all!

106

GO TO A HOME IMPROVEMENT STORE'S WORKSHOP

These stores often have classes like painting tips, how to install a tile backsplash, etc. See which workshops they are offering and pick one you could implement together in your home.

107

HOST A DINNER PARTY

STAY IN

Invite another couple or two for dinner. You can go all out and make preparing for the party into a special bonding time for you and your spouse; or, you can host potluck style and have each couple contribute part of the meal - you provide the main dish, ask someone to bring dessert, etc. Either way, try to enjoy the process of getting ready together instead of turning it into a stressful and frantic cleaning frenzy!

108

PLAY TENNIS

GO OUT

Many rec centers or college courts have racquets available to borrow, if you don't own them yourselves. You can also search for racquets at yard sales. Tennis can be challenging! If you get discouraged or overwhelmed, try seeing how many hits you can get back and forth. Keep trying to beat your last record - great for building teamwork!

109

CREATE A DRAWING TOGETHER

This is like that game when you create a story, one sentence at a time! Get a large canvas or sketch pad and take turns drawing one small piece of the picture at a time. For example, you start with a box (maybe it will become a house), but then it's his turn and he adds an antenna like it's an old box TV! Keep drawing items until you have an entire scene -- no fair planning ahead or coaching each other. It's fun to see how you interpret what the other person draws.

110

RIDE BIKES

If you don't have any, see if there is a local place that rents them. Low cost, high quality bicycles can also be found at garage sales or thrift stores, or maybe you can borrow from a friend. If you're feeling extra adventurous, try biking on mountain bike trails or doing a midnight ride (in a well lit area, and with headlights and reflectors on your bikes, of course!).

111

GO PEOPLE WATCHING

Create stories for each of the people you see, or choose two people who are talking and make up voices for them. It's fun to see what your spouse notices about people first, or what features and mannerisms stand out most to him.

112

PLAY THE TRADE-UP GAME

This game is easy, but might take one (or both) of you out of your comfort zone! Start with a small object, like a quarter or a paper clip. Go to your neighbor's house (or a nearby neighborhood if that feels less awkward), ring the doorbell, and ask what they will trade for. The only rule is that it has to be either bigger or better! Maybe they will offer you a coffee mug. Now, head to the next house and ask what they will trade for your mug! Keep going until you have something you can use to enjoy the rest of your date.

GO TO AN ESTATE AUCTION

It can be fun just to see all the things someone owns, and also a great way to pick up new furniture or decor for your home. Keep your eyes open for one in a really ritzy neighborhood and enjoy the experience of exploring the life of a stranger.

MAKE TIE-DYE SHIRTS

Choose colors you both love and research different ways to tie the shirts to make designs you will love. You can also think outside the box and branch out from the t-shirt; instead try making tie-dye pillowcases, sheets, or even socks.

115

TAKE FLOWERS TO YOUR LOCAL NURSING HOME

GO OUT

The residents will absolutely love the visitors, and the flowers are a nice way to bring some beauty to their day. Call ahead to find out the best time to visit, and maybe ask about a resident you could spend time with, who doesn't have many visitors or family.

116

HIT SATURDAY MORNING YARD SALES

GO OUT

Start the morning with coffee together and research neighborhoods that have several sales nearby. Don't forget to pick up cash beforehand, in case you find a treasure you weren't expecting!

117

MESSAGE IN A BOTTLE

Each of you, write a letter to your spouse, then seal them in a bottle. Save them for one, five, or ten years and look forward to opening them and see how much you've changed and grown.

118

DANCE IN THE RAIN

Okay, you can't plan ahead on this one, but tuck it away in your mind for now. The next time it's raining and the kids are already in bed, run outside and dance together. Splash in the puddles, and kiss the raindrops off your hubby's nose. Dry off and warm up together with a cup of warm tea.

INDOOR ROCK CLIMBING

Call ahead to a local climbing gym and ask if they have any special deals or days that are less expensive. Climbing can be a real physical challenge, but it's great practice for encouraging each other as you cheer your spouse to the top!

' JUST CHOOSE ONE ' FOOD DATE

Pick a mutual favorite food item, like pizza, ice cream, or cupcakes. Then choose three or four places that serve your chosen food and go on a taste tour, trying a serving at each place.

121

FIND YOUR LOVE LANGUAGE

The test can be found online, and it's pretty quick and simple to take. Compare your results, and talk about what makes you feel the most loved.

122

DIY MUG

Everyone is decorating mugs today! Why not decorate one for each other? Take it a step further and decorate a whole place setting. We've had the best luck with using Oil-Based Paint Markers so they don't rub off. Just choose plain white mugs (and bowls and plates, if you want!), your favorite colors, and get to work.

WRITE AND ILLUSTRATE A CHILDREN'S BOOK

Choose one of your favorite stories and turn it into a short book for your kiddos (or future ones!). It doesn't have to be fancy. Just use plain paper. Folded in half and stapled makes a simple book with plenty of room for writing and drawing. It doesn't matter if you aren't artistic! Your kids will love it regardless of the level of skill.

124

TREASURE HUNT

Create a treasure hunt for each other. Divide the house into 2 separate areas, or someone can create one outside while the other creates it inside. Or, if only one of you has time to prepare, make a treasure hunt and enjoy watching your spouse track down the clues. Wrap a box for the first clue which leads him to the bathroom closet; there he gets another box with the next clue and so on. At the end of the hunt, have a special, romantic gift ready!

125

ROOT BEER FLOATS

You can't go wrong with this one. It's simple, it's delicious, and it makes the perfect dessert for a fun night! Pop in a movie or just sit and chat while you enjoy the root beer floats! Don't overthink this date; just have good ole' simple fun!

126

PLAY DARTS

If you can get away from home, find a local bar with a dart board. Otherwise, get one for the basement and set it up somewhere the kids won't see it. It can be your own little secret with each other!

127

DECORATE COOKIES TOGETHER

Of course, sugar cookies with icing and sprinkles are an easy way to do this. However, there are so many different kinds of cookies! If one of you has a favorite, make those and then find a creative way to decorate them.

128

ENJOY BRUNCH OR BREAKFAST AT A LOCAL CAFÉ

Get a full breakfast and coffee (or mimosas!) and be sure to sit outside. There's something special about eating outside in the morning air together - it's both romantic and energizing!!

129

ROAD TRIP TO A NEARBY TOWN

Walk the "down town" strip, no matter how small it might look; or find the local historic district. While you're shopping the stores and boutiques, ask the owners their favorite local eating places and head to the most authentic one you can find.

130

START A TWO-MEMBER BOOK CLUB

Choose a book for each month, read it separately, on your own time, and then go on a date at the end of the month to discuss it. You can pick old classics, marriage books, or hot new novels. Mix it up, and get ready to compare notes!

131

ETHNIC RESTAURANT EXPERIENCE

GO OUT

Go to an ethnic restaurant you haven't visited before.
Research the country beforehand and dream about what you
would do if you ever visited there together. Try to order a meal
that is an authentic dish from that country.

132

MAKE YOUR OWN VIDEO

STAY IN

**Sing a song together, lip sync, or do some stand up comedy
or a skit.** Edit it together and enjoy watching it
and laughing at yourselves!

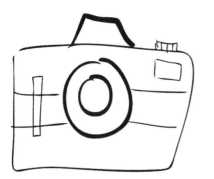

133

TRUCK-BED STARGAZING

 GO OUT

Rent a truck or borrow from a friend. Fill the back with blankets and pillows and go star gazing. Choose a clear night and find a place to park as far from the city lights as possible. (Maybe you have a friend in the country whose driveway is available.) Use a phone app to identify constellations and choose your favorite one.

134

RIDE GO-KARTS

GO OUT

A lot of newer places will have go-karts that cater to adults. The courses are built for speed and the go-karts are big enough that you won't feel like you have to fold in half to drive! Race each other a few times - best two out of three! Get snow cones or other throwback snacks together afterwards.

135

TAKE A CLASS TOGETHER

Research the colleges or trade schools near you to see if they are offering any courses that fit your interests. Often, mini weekend lectures will be offered that might be easier to fit into your schedule, time-wise. Ideas include everything from photography to learning computer programming skills. Choose something that is new for both of you, and enjoy learning together!

136

100 THINGS I LOVE ABOUT YOU

Take an evening and each write out 100 things you love about each other. Frame your lists next to each other and add a copy to your Smash Book. Be creative, silly, and genuine - you'll be surprised how quickly 100 things come to mind!

137

VISIT A LOCAL FAIR OR CARNIVAL

Ride the ferris wheel and eat funnel cake! Ask a stranger to snap a photo of you while you're there. Try to position yourself with the ferris wheel in the background to capture the fun memory!

138

RELIVE YOUR WEDDING CAKE SMASH

Bake and decorate a cake together and then feed/smash each other your first bite! Help each other clean up and then enjoy the rest of the cake together.

GO ON A HOLIDAY LIGHT TOUR

Larger towns often have these at local attractions, but if you can't find one, then drive around nearby neighborhoods and try to find the best decorated house for the holidays!

140

KARAOKE NIGHT

Most people either love or hate karaoke! If you've never done it, I encouraged you to try and find a place and go together. If you are still building up confidence, start by having a karaoke night at home. Look-up online music videos with lyrics on the screen. Make a DIY mic, and sing your hearts out together. Duets are especially fun!

141

SLINGSHOT DATE

 STAY IN

Build your own slingshots and grab some empty tin cans and see who has the better aim.

142

HOT AIR BALLOON RIDE

 GO OUT

This is one of those bucket list items every couple should do! Do a quick internet search to find one close to you and make a day of it.

VISIT AN ANIMAL SHELTER

Play with or walk pets at a local animal shelter.
Be careful though - if you do this too often, you may want to adopt one yourselves!

DOLLAR STORE DATE

There are so many ways to have fun at the dollar store.
Here's one: Each choose a gift for your spouse and spend another $1 on a gift bag or something used to wrap it!

TREAT YOURSELF TO A COUPLES' MASSAGE

Keep your eyes open for deals at local massage parlors and enjoy getting pampered together.

146

START A WORDLESS BLOG

Upload one photo every day with a fun post title, no description or writing necessary. Plan to do this for an entire year. Eventually, it will be a great online journal of your year together that you can look back to and remember.

FIND A LOCAL COUPON BOOK

Flip through it until you find something you love. Or leave it up to chance by flipping through with your eyes shut and randomly landing on a page.

GO TO A CAR SHOW

Try finding a show with vintage cars or cool sports cars. If your man loves cars, let him teach you something new or if neither of you love cars, it can still be fun to walk around and listen in as other people talk about what's under the hood! Don't forget to take a photo next to your favorite one.

TAKE A TRAIL RIDE

During the "off season", many camps or resorts will offer inexpensive horse trail rides. In late fall or early spring, put on your favorite old jeans and enjoy the experience of horseback riding together!

GO SKIING OR SNOWBOARDING

If you live near mountains, this one is definitely a must; but even if you don't, don't dismiss the idea quite yet! There are many places that "make snow" so there's enough to ski! Or, if your budget allows, plan a special trip to the mountains and enjoy the slopes.

151

BUILD A HOMEMADE FORT

Challenge yourself to use every single pillow and blanket.
Enjoy being kids together for the night. Once it's done,
you can snuggle-up inside and play board games
or read books together.

152

GRILL AT YOUR LOCAL PARK

**Go back to basics and make simple hamburgers, or get
more fancy with teriyaki chicken breasts or marinated
shish kabobs.**

153

PUT TOGETHER A PUZZLE

Choose one that you can complete in one evening together. Even more fun would be to have a puzzle made out of a favorite photo of the two of you together!

154

GO TO THE ZOO

Talk about your favorite animals, then and now. Maybe it's changed as you've aged. Tell stories about childhood pets and don't forget to buy a favorite zoo postcard for your Smash Book!

LOOK THROUGH OLD PICTURE ALBUMS

You might have to borrow old albums or scrapbooks from your parents so you can go way back. Find photos of each other from the same age (for example, when you were both 5 years old) and make a copy of them for your Smash Book. Compare how differently or similarly you looked!

PLAY BACKYARD GAMES

STAY IN

Horse Shoes, Croquet, and Corn Hole are some of our favorites. Ladder Golf is also really fun, and it could be a fun date to make a set together, using PVC pipe, golf balls, and rope.

FIND AN OBSERVATORY & LOOK AT THE STARS

These places often have free nights or nights open to the public. Start by trying a local university or science museum.

DIY FONDUE NIGHT

Buy chocolate chips and your favorite fondue items, like marshmallows, rice krispie treats, strawberries, or pretzels. Simply melt the chocolate chips on the stove and dip your items in for a yummy treat! You can also do a meal fondue by boiling tasty broth and dipping chunks of chicken, beef, and vegetables in for a few minutes. If you enjoy this, invest in some fun skewers and make it a regular date activity!

159

FIND HIDDEN TREASURES IN AN ANTIQUE MALL OR PAWN SHOP

Wander through the aisles looking for items that look like they come with an interesting history or remind you of your spouse.

160

TAKE A POTTERY OR OTHER ART CLASS

Most classes like this will meet for several weeks. Choose one that interests both of you and enjoy a month or more of weekly date nights while you learn a new form of art.

GO TO A SHOOTING RANGE

If guns aren't your style, find an archery range or paintball course where you can play. (See date #166.)

MAKE A SPECIAL PLAYLIST

STAY IN

Put your heads together to create a great list of songs that you both love. Next time he's at work and you're at home doing the dishes, turn on the music and let a smile come to your face knowing that you're both enjoying the same songs. You can also use this list for future road trips, because you're sure to both love everything that plays!

THREE DAY WEEKEND

Take full advantage of your next three day weekend and plan a mini vacation! It can be as extravagant as you want or super budget savvy, anything from booking last minute air tickets (you may be able to find a random good deal if you're up for going anywhere) to camping out at a local state park. I think you'll be surprised how much fun you can have in three days, regardless of budget.

Note: if you have kids, see if grandma and grandpa or some trusted friends can watch them.

SURPRISE DATE

This is especially fun for married couples! Pick a time and place to meet, get ready in separate parts of the house, and head to the restaurant in separate cars so you don't know what each other looks like until you get there! Go that extra mile and look great, like you would for a first date. Ladies, invite a friend to help with your hair. Men, stop by the store and buy a new shirt; or take a quick trip to the hair salon and surprise her for the date.

LOCAL TOURS

Tour a microbrewery, historic home, chocolate factory, or other local landmark. I think you'll be surprised by what you find around you.

PLAY PAINTBALL

Find a local course where you can go, invite another couple, or two, to join you. If you're a little nervous, let your man "protect" you through the course or try slingshot paintball instead.

PLAN A REALISTIC DREAM VACATION

Where do you want to go? What do you want to see while you're there? Get online and do some searches, maybe even order some tour books from the area. Make it something realistic enough that you can visualize yourself saving-up and affording it at some point in your future. When the time comes for the trip, you will know all the perfect places to go! It might be a trip you can plan for a milestone anniversary, like a five- or ten-year anniversary. That will give you time to save money and enjoy dreaming about it for a while before it happens. Make sure you write down all your ideas and plans in your Smash Book (page #109).

168

SUMMER MOVIES AT THE PARK

If your local town doesn't have them, search your neighboring towns to find one that does! Bring blankets or lawn chairs and enjoy the long summer night together.

169

PLAY CATCH

Although it sounds almost too simple, there is something really fun about it. Take two gloves and a baseball to the backyard or a park and toss it back and forth. Move further apart as you get warmed up, or let him help you learn better throwing form. You could also gather a few more couples together and play kickball or touch football.

170

OPEN HOUSE DATE

GO OUT

Go to open houses, even if you're not currently in the market for a house. Make notes of what you like about each house and piece them together to figure out what your dream house ultimately looks like. Jot down all your notes on page #110 in your Smash Book. Stop by a paint store and select a few paint samples, colors you want in your future house, and include those too!

171

HOUSE HUNTING FROM HOME

STAY IN

Expand on your dream house from the Open House Date (#170). Sit down together and look at houses online. Don't just search your city; search anywhere in the U.S. or maybe even the world. Make notes about what you love about certain houses and which cities are your favorite. Dream big and create a vision together of what you want your next house or dream house to be like. Keep adding all your thoughts to your Smash Book.

DRAW BLUE PRINTS TO YOUR DREAM HOUSE

These don't have to be formal, architectural drawings.
Just grab a piece of scrap paper and start brainstorming together! Add on rooms as you go. Talk about your priorities and styles. Do you like an open floor plan; or would you prefer the intimacy of more closed-off rooms? Once you have a rough draft made, either perfect it by hand or find a program online to help design the floor plan. Paper clip it in the back of your Smash Book, tucked away for 'one day'.

BUILD CARD HOUSES

You'll need a few decks of cards. Clear the dining room table and see who can build the highest house; or work together on a giant card house! Make sure you snap a picture! You can also take a few cards (maybe the 2 from the very top) and tape them in your Smash Book with your picture. You'll have an incomplete deck, but it will be worth it for making the Smash Book look awesome next to the photo!

174

THE SELFIE DATE

GO OUT

This super fun date idea is simple! Just take selfies all night long. Snap a shot in the bedroom while you're getting ready and one in the car before you hit the road. If you're feeling adventurous, get a selfie with the waitress at the restaurant or the guy at the movie ticket counter. Final step? Order prints of your favorites and enjoy them together.

175

MAKE A DATE JAR TOGETHER

STAY IN

A beautiful combination of his and her date ideas will make your jar one of a kind. Each of you write a few of your favorite dates from this past year, and slip them into the jar so you can experience them again! Dating should never have an end!

HOW TO MAKE A DATE JAR

YOU'LL NEED:

- Wide Mouth Mason Jar (keep it simple; or for a little extra pizzazz, decorate it!)
- Strips of Colored Paper

MAKE YOUR DATE JAR:

1. Cut an even number of strips for each person, pinks for her, blues for him.

2. Now grab all of your color pieces and split your pile in half, making 2 stacks. On the first stack you are going to fill the strips with your favorite date ideas, writing one idea per strip. For the second stack you are going to fill the strips with ideas on what you think HE WILL LOVE. {Example: My first stack included: making dinner together, picnic in the park and game night. For my second stack I wrote ideas like: movie theater date, a drive around town listening to our favorite tunes, Redbox and pizza at home — things I know he loves!}

3. *Optional:* You can also add yellow strips into your jar for at-home date ideas. Nights you can't find a babysitter for the kids or just want to stay in, pick a yellow date idea out of the jar.

4. Fold all the strips in half and stuff them in your jar. Take turns, every other week, pulling out an idea. Alternate blue, pink, blue, pink. Whatever the date idea says, you have to do!

5. After the date, tape the strip from the date into your Smash Book *(that you made in date #5)* and scribble a note with your favorite part of the night next to it.

CONCLUSION

This book might be finished, but your date jar will keep you going! And of course, you can also come back and flip through the book for inspiration at anytime! Choose one date that was your favorite, or just open the book and do the first date your eyes see.

If you had a blast through this book, we hope you'll share the love with your friends. Surprise them with their own book, "just because!" Give it as a gift whenever you have a wedding or engagement party to go to. When giving as a gift, paper clip $20 to the inside cover to start their date fund. It's a fun extra touch.

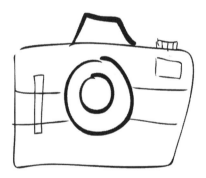

Make sure to use the hashtag

#175DATEIDEAS

when you share on Instagram, Facebook, or Twitter.

SMASH BOOK!

#175DATEIDEAS

LOVE LETTERS

DATE #5

love

DATE #5

BUCKET LISTS

Mr. _____
_____
_____
_____

Mrs. _____
_____
_____
_____

Mr. & Mrs. _____
_____
_____
_____

DATE #91

DREAM VACATION

DATE #167

DREAM HOME

DATES #170, 171, 172

H♥me

ME and YOU

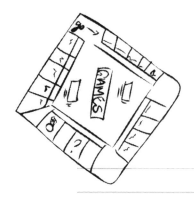

LOVE

GO OUT

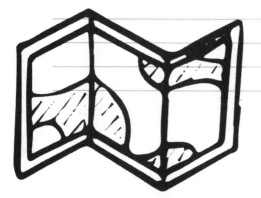

ME and YOU

Made in the USA
Middletown, DE
09 December 2017